101 More Things To Do With Ramen Noodles

101 More Things To Do With Ramen Noodles

BY
TONI PATRICK

GIBBS SMITH
TO ENRICH AND INSPIRE HUMANKIND

First Edition
20 19 18 17   20 19 18 17 16 15 14 13 12 11 10 9 8 7 6 5

Published by
Gibbs Smith
P.O. Box 667
Layton, Utah 84041

1.800.835.4993 orders
www.gibbs-smith.com

Consulting editor: Stephanie Ashcraft
Printed and bound in Korea
Gibbs Smith books are printed on either recycled, 100% post-
consumer waste, FSC-certified papers or on paper produced from
a 100% certified sustainable forest/controlled wood source.

Library of Congress Cataloging-in-Publication Data

Patrick, Toni.
   101 more things to do with ramen noodles / Toni Patrick. — 1st ed.
      p. cm.
   ISBN 978-1-4236-1636-8
   1. Cooking (Pasta) 2. Noodles. I. Title. II. Title: One hundred
one more things to do with ramen noodles. III. Title: One
hundred and one more things to do with ramen noodles.
   TX809.M17P3747 2011
   641.8'22—dc22
                                        2010035247

I would like to give an extra special
thanks to my mom, who has always
helped, supported, and inspired me.
I love you!

To both my moms, Georgie Patrick
and Cyndi Duncan, this book would
never have been written had you not
given me a shot to begin with.

To my daughter, Robbi, I love you
and cherish you and thank you for
sharing the ramen with the dog.
He is now a ramen lover, too!

To the rest of my family,
thanks for your love and support.

And to my grandmother, Geneva Hewitt,
I will love you and honor you for eternity.

CONTENTS

Helpful Hints 9

Breakfast

Quick and Easy Breakfast Ramen 12 • Bacon Fried Ramen 13 • Spinach and Eggs Ramen 14 • Fried Ramen and Eggs 15 • Breakfast Ramen 16 • Cheesy Omelet 17 • Breakfast Casserole 18 • Ricotta Frittata 19

Soups

Mexican Ramen Soup 22 • Ham and Black-Eyed Peas 23 • Asian Ramen Noodle Soup 24 • Mayan Soup 25 • Spicy Shrimp and Noodle Soup 26 • Corn Chowder 27 • Chicken Soup 28 • Miso Ramen 29 • Curried Chicken Soup 30 • Tuna Noodle Stew 31 • Chicken Chile Ramen 32

Salads

Broccoli Slaw 34 • Oriental Chicken Salad 35 • Cole Slaw 36 • Mandarin Salad 37 • Nutty-Grape Salad 38 • Quick Chicken Salad 39 • Tangerine Chicken Salad 40 • Sprouting Ramen Salad 41 • Polish Ramen Salad 42 • Fruit Salad 43 • Chicken Fajita Ramen Salad 44 • Tofu Salad 45 • Oriental Salad 46

Sides

Grilled Ramen 48 • Chinese Fried Noodles 49 • Stuffed Tomatoes 50 • Tuna Noodle Spread 51 • Baked Ramen Cakes 52 • Sweet and Salty Ramen 53 • Twisted Ramen 54 • Ramen Pancakes 55

Casseroles

Chicken Casserole 58 • Chicken Broccoli Casserole 59 • Ramen Noodle Casserole 60 • Mexican Ramen Casserole 61 • Cheesy Turkey

*Casserole 62 • Layered Ramen 63 • Broccoli and Ham Casserole 64
• Tuna Ramen Casserole 65 • Tomato-Basil Turkey Casserole 66*

Vegetable

*Bok Choy Ramen 68 • Spinach Parmesan Ramen 69 • Asian Noodle
Toss 70 • Broccoli and Ramen Noodles 71 • Yakisoba 72 • Pad Thai 73
• Ohm Raisu Ramen 74 • Olive and Red Pepper Ramen 75 • Spicy Lime
Ramen 76 • Italian Ramen Patties 77 • Mushroom and Zucchini Ramen 78*

Poultry

*Herbed Chicken 80 • Garlic Chicken Toss 81 • Thai Chicken 82
• Caesar Chicken Ramen 83 • Honey Grilled Chicken 84 • Turkey-
Pasta Pie 85 • Turkey Gravy Noodles 86 • Turkey Ramen 87 • Leftover
Thanksgiving Fried Ramen 88 • Pesto Turkey and Pasta 89*

Meats

*Meatballs and Pineapple Ramen 92 • Ramen Rolled Steak 93 • Yatsobi 94
• Crock-Pot Beef and Noodles 95 • Stuffed Bell Peppers 96 • Gingered
Pork and Ramen 97 • Oriental Hot Dogs 98 • Spicy Sausage Ramen 99
• Hot and Sour Ramen 100 • Pork Skillet 101 • Pepperoni Pizza 102*

Seafood

*Garlic Shrimp Ramen 104 • Crab Lo Mein 105 • Smoked Mussel
Ramen 106 • Teriyaki Tuna Ramen 107 • Salmon Ramen 108 • Swedish
Ramen 109 • Cajun Seafood Noodles 110 • Ramen Clam Chowder
Pie 111 • Spinach Crab Ramen 112 • Coconut Curry Shrimp 113*

Dessert

*Chocolate Cherry Cakes 116 • Chocolate Ramen Balls 117 • Jiggly Ramen 118
• Quick and Easy Fried Ice Cream 119 • Choco-Banana Crunch Cakes 120
• Chocolate Ramen 121 • Strawberry Ramen Ice Cream 122 • Caramel
Ramen 123 • White Chocolate Ramen Cookie 124 • Thin Mint on a Stick 125*

HELPFUL HINTS

1. Extra uses for ramen flavor packets:
   - Add to water while preparing any noodle or rice for extra flavor
   - Use instead of bouillon—add 1 packet for every 2 cups of water
   - Use to flavor gravy—stir into pan drippings along with flour or whisk in water for use instead of stock
   - Shake and bake for potatoes
   - Cutlet, chop, and fish coating—mix 1 packet per 2 tablespoons of flour for coating
   - Mix with bread crumbs for frying
   - Season ground meat for burgers, meatballs, and meat loaf—mix 1 packet per pound of ground meat
   - Seasoning rubs for chicken, steaks, and pork chops

2. Check ramen packaging for vegetarian or vegan manufacturers. Just because it is labeled as vegetable ramen does not mean animal products were not used in the manufacturing process.

3. The ramen noodles are finished cooking when they turn yellow and begin to separate.

4. Do not overcook ramen noodles. They will become mush.

5. Salt lovers beware. Taste before throwing in those extra dashes—the seasoning packets are salty.

6. To reduce fat and calories, substitute reduced-fat foods such as skim milk, light or fat-free sour cream, and light or fat-free cream cheese.

7. 1 clove garlic equals 1 teaspoon minced garlic. This is much more cost effective than bottled minced garlic.

8. $1/4$ cup fresh minced onion equals 2 tablespoons dried minced onion.

9. $^1/_4$ cup fresh herbs equals 1 tablespoon dried herbs.

10. Fresh or frozen vegetables, steamed, can be substituted for canned vegetables.

11. As always, be creative! Most ingredients can be adjusted to your own liking.

BREAKFAST

QUICK AND EASY BREAKFAST RAMEN

	water
1 package	**vegetable ramen noodles,** with seasoning packet
4	**tomato slices**
1	**green onion,** sliced
2	**eggs,** beaten

Put just enough water in a small saucepan to cover the brick of ramen noodles. When the water comes to a boil, stir in seasoning packet and add the brick of noodles. Cover with tomatoes, sprinkle with onion, and pour eggs on the top. Put on a lid and wait for it to boil just enough for the egg to cook to your liking. Makes 1–2 servings.

BACON FRIED RAMEN

4 slices	**raw bacon,** cut in $^1/_4$-inch pieces
3 cups	**water**
2 packages	**any flavor ramen noodles**
	salt and pepper, to taste
pinch	**red pepper flakes**
1 teaspoon	**soy sauce**
1	**egg**

Place bacon into a large nonstick frying pan and let cook slowly on medium-low heat. In a medium saucepan, bring water to a boil. Add noodles and cook for 3 minutes.

Quickly drain the noodles completely and pour into a bowl of ice cold water to stop the cooking process. Stir the noodles with your hands until they are cold.

Once the bacon has finished cooking, drain the chilled noodles and combine with the bacon in the pan. Turn the stove up to medium-high heat. Season noodles and bacon with salt, pepper, red pepper flakes, and soy sauce. Continue to cook for 2–3 minutes.

Move noodles to one side of the pan. Crack the egg into open side of pan, mixing the egg in the pan and let it cook for 1–2 minutes. Cut up the egg and stir in with bacon and noodles. Continue cooking and turning for 3–4 more minutes. Makes 1–2 servings.

SPINACH AND EGGS RAMEN

2 cups	**water**
I package	**chicken ramen noodles,** with seasoning packet
¼ cup	**frozen spinach,** thawed and drained
dash	**soy sauce**
dash	**rice vinegar**
I	**egg**

In a small saucepan, bring water to a boil, add noodles, and cook for 3 minutes or until done. Drain and set aside.

In a frying pan over medium heat, combine the spinach, soy sauce, vinegar, and about ¼–⅓ of the seasoning packet; toss.

Beat egg in a bowl and then add to the pan; continue cooking until egg begins to set. Add noodles and cook until noodles begin to brown, stirring regularly. Makes I–2 servings.

FRIED RAMEN AND EGGS

2 cups	**water**
I package	**any flavor ramen noodles,** with seasoning packet
2 dashes	**sesame oil**
$^1/_4$ cup	**cooking oil**
I tablespoon	**finely chopped onion**
I tablespoon	**finely chopped green bell pepper**
I tablespoon	**finely chopped red bell pepper**
2	**eggs**
I tablespoon	**soy sauce**

In a small saucepan, bring water to a boil and cook noodles, until tender but still firm; drain. Toss noodles with sesame oil and half of seasoning packet (save rest of packet for something else); set noodles aside.

Heat just enough cooking oil to cover bottom of frying pan over medium-low heat until hot. Add noodles, spreading out carefully. Cook until they begin to crisp on the bottom, turn over carefully with spatula and separate them slightly, adding a bit more oil if they start to stick. Sprinkle onion and bell peppers over the noodles. Beat eggs with soy sauce.

Pour eggs over noodles and cook, mixing gently with a fork or spatula, until done to your liking. Makes 1–2 servings.

BREAKFAST RAMEN

2 cups	**water**
I package	**chicken ramen noodles**
2	**eggs,** beaten
1/4 cup	**grated cheddar cheese**
4 slices	**bacon,** chopped
4	**large mushrooms,** diced
I	**small tomato,** diced

In a small saucepan, boil water. Add noodles and cook for 3 minutes; drain and place in a large bowl.

Beat eggs and pour over noodles; toss. Add cheese and toss again.

In a large frying pan over medium heat, cook bacon pieces until bacon starts to crisp, stirring regularly to keep pieces separated. Add mushrooms and saute for I minute. Add tomato and continue to cook until bacon is done. Add noodles and toss until evenly distributed. Cook over medium heat for 3–4 minutes stirring to ensure all the egg has been cooked completely. Noodles will begin to brown. Makes I–2 servings.

CHEESY OMELET

2 cups	**water**
I package	**vegetable ramen noodles,** with seasoning packet
I tablespoon	**butter or margarine**
2	**eggs**
$^1/_8$ cup	**milk**
2 slices	**Velveeta cheese**

In a small saucepan, bring water to a boil. Add noodles and cook for 2 minutes; drain.

Put butter in a medium microwave-safe bowl, microwave for 20–30 seconds, or until melted. Add eggs, milk, and $^1/_4$ of the seasoning packet; whisk to combine. Add noodles and toss.

Pour contents into a frying pan heated to medium-high and cover. Flip omelets when underside begins to separate from pan and becomes brown. Top with cheese and return cover. Once bottom begins to brown, fold over and serve. Makes I–2 servings.

BREAKFAST CASSEROLE

9	**eggs,** separated
I teaspoon plus 2 tablespoons	**vegetable oil,** divided
I teaspoon	**sugar**
3 cups	**water**
2 packages	**mushroom or chicken ramen noodles,** with seasoning packets
I teaspoon	**soy sauce**
3	**green onions,** sliced and divided
I (8-ounce) package	**sliced fresh mushrooms**
I teaspoon	**ginger**
I teaspoon	**garlic powder**

Preheat oven to 350 degrees. Prepare an 8 x 8-inch glass baking dish with nonstick cooking spray. In a small mixing bowl, whisk 3 egg yolks with 9 egg whites. Beat in I teaspoon oil and sugar to egg mixture; set aside. In large saucepan, boil water. Add noodles and cook 3 minutes.

Heat a medium frying pan over medium heat with 2 tablespoons oil and soy sauce. Setting $\frac{1}{3}$ of the onions to the side for topping later, saute the mushrooms and onions in the pan. Stir in ginger and garlic. Saute until mushrooms begin to darken a little; remove from heat.

Drain the cooked noodles and then stir in one of the seasoning packets. Add the contents of the frying pan to the saucepan of noodles and mix well. Slowly add the egg mixture into the saucepan, stirring well. Replace saucepan over medium heat for a couple of minutes, until the liquid egg around the mixture begins to form tiny bubbles.

Immediately transfer the mixture to the baking dish. Top with the reserved onions. Bake approximately 15 minutes, or until top begins to brown and eggs are cooked. Remove from oven and allow to cool completely before serving. Makes 6–8 servings.

RICOTTA FRITTATA

6 cups	**water**
2 cups	**frozen green peas**
3 packages	**mushroom ramen noodles,** with seasoning packets
I container (15 ounces)	**part-skim ricotta cheese**
3	**eggs**
$\frac{1}{2}$ cup	**milk**
$\frac{1}{2}$ cup	**grated Parmesan cheese**
$\frac{1}{4}$ teaspoon	**pepper**
I can (14.5 ounces)	**Italian style diced tomatoes**

Preheat oven to 400 degrees. Lightly prepare a 13 x 9-inch baking dish with nonstick cooking spray.

In a large saucepan, bring water to a boil. Add peas and return to a boil. Break up noodles as directed on package and add to pan. Cook 3 minutes, stirring occasionally, or until noodles and peas are tender; drain.

Mix ricotta, eggs, milk, cheese, pepper, and 2 seasoning packets in a large bowl until blended. Stir in noodles and peas. Transfer mixture to baking dish and spread evenly. Bake about 20 minutes or until set. Heat tomatoes in the microwave for I minute or until hot. Spoon over frittata. Cut in squares to serve. Makes 6 servings.

SOUPS

MEXICAN RAMEN SOUP

3 cups	**water**
1	**lime,** juiced
4 tablespoons	**chili powder**
1 teaspoon	**garlic powder**
dash	**hot sauce**
1/4 teaspoon	**chopped cilantro**
2 packages	**chicken ramen noodles,** with seasoning packets
1	**chicken breast,** cooked and cubed
1 can (16 ounces)	**corn,** drained
1 can (16 ounces)	**black beans,** drained and rinsed
1	**medium avocado,** diced
1/4 cup	**sour cream**
	tortilla chips, crushed

In a large saucepan add water, lime juice, chili powder, garlic, hot sauce, cilantro, and seasoning packets. Bring to a boil over medium heat. Add noodles, chicken, corn, and beans. Allow to cook for 3 minutes. Portion into bowls and top with avocado, sour cream, and tortilla chips. Makes 2–4 servings.

HAM AND BLACK-EYED PEAS

1 tablespoon	**vegetable oil**
2 cups	**chopped collard greens**
1/4 cup	**chopped green onions,** divided
1 clove	**garlic,** chopped
6 cups	**water**
2 packages	**pork ramen noodles,** with seasoning packets
1 cup	**diced ham**
1 can (15 ounces)	**black-eyed peas,** drained and rinsed
2 tablespoons	**chopped cilantro**

Add oil to a large saucepan over medium-high heat. When the oil is warm, add collard greens, half of the onions, and garlic. Stir-fry for 2 minutes. Don't overcook; the collards should still be bright green. Add water and seasoning packets and bring to a boil. Add noodles, ham, and black-eyed peas. Allow to simmer for 3 minutes. Portion and garnish with reserved onion and cilantro. Makes 4–6 servings.

ASIAN RAMEN NOODLE SOUP

6 cups	**water**
2 packages	**chicken ramen noodles,** with seasoning packets
4 ounces	**cooked boneless pork loin,** sliced
3/4 cup	**thinly sliced mushrooms**
1/2 cup	**cubed firm tofu**
3 tablespoons	**white vinegar**
3 tablespoons	**sherry**
1 tablespoon	**soy sauce**
1/2 teaspoon	**ground red pepper**
1	**egg,** beaten
1/4 cup	**chopped green onions**

Bring the water and both seasoning packets to a boil in large saucepan over high heat; add pork, mushrooms, and tofu. Reduce heat to medium-low; simmer, covered, 5 minutes. Stir in vinegar, sherry, soy sauce, and red pepper. Return broth mixture to a boil over high heat and add noodles, add more water to ensure noodles are covered. Cook for 3 minutes. Slowly stir in egg and onions. Makes 4–6 servings.

MAYAN SOUP

6 cups	**water**
2 packages	**chicken ramen noodles,** with seasoning packets
1	**lime,** juiced
$1/8$ teaspoon	**pepper**
1 teaspoon	**chopped parsley**
2	**green onions,** chopped

Bring water, seasoning packets, lime juice, pepper, parsley, and onions to a boil in large saucepan over high heat. Add noodles and cook for 3 minutes. Makes 4–6 servings.

SPICY SHRIMP
AND NOODLE SOUP

1 tablespoon	**lemon juice**
1/4 teaspoon	**chili powder**
1/4 teaspoon	**ground cumin**
1/8 teaspoon	**pepper**
1 pound	**ready-to-cook shrimp**
6 cups	**water**
2 packages	**oriental ramen noodles,** with seasoning packets
2 cups	**salsa**
1 can (15 ounces)	**black beans,** rinsed and drained
1 can (15 ounces)	**corn,** drained
1	**green onion,** sliced

In a medium bowl, combine lemon juice, chili powder, cumin, and pepper; add shrimp and toss to coat. Let stand 20 minutes.

In a large saucepan bring the water and seasoning packets to boil. Add noodles, shrimp, salsa, beans, corn, and onion heat though until shrimp turn pink, about 3 minutes. Makes 6–8 servings.

CORN CHOWDER

1 package	**any flavor ramen noodles**
1 package (1.8 ounces)	**dry vegetable soup mix**
2 cups	**milk**
1 cup	**water**
1 can (15 ounces)	**creamed corn**

Combine all ingredients in a large microwave-safe bowl. Cover and cook on high for 8 minutes. Makes 2–4 servings.

CHICKEN SOUP

2	**sweet potatoes,** cubed
1	**onion,** chopped
1 bag (16 ounces)	**baby carrots**
6	**boneless, skinless chicken thighs,** cubed
1/2 teaspoon	**dried thyme leaves**
1/8 teaspoon	**pepper**
6 cups	**water,** divided
2 packages	**chicken ramen noodles,** with seasoning packets
2	**bay leaves**

In a 4- to 5-quart crock-pot, layer the sweet potatoes, onion, carrots, and chicken. Sprinkle with thyme and pepper.

In a small bowl, blend 1 cup water and seasoning packets. Pour over chicken and vegetables, add bay leaves and remaining water. Cover and cook on low for 7–9 hours or until vegetables and chicken are tender. Remove and discard bay leaves. Stir in noodles and cover. Cook on high 10–12 minutes or until noodles are tender, stirring once during cooking. Makes 6–8 servings.

MISO RAMEN

2 teaspoons	**olive oil**
1 teaspoon	**minced fresh ginger**
1 clove	**garlic,** minced
2 ounces	**ground pork**
2	**carrots,** cut into thin strips
1 cup	**bean sprouts,** rinsed
1 cup	**chopped cabbage**
4 cups	**water**
2 packages	**chicken ramen noodles,** with seasoning packets
1 teaspoon	**sugar**
2 teaspoons	**light soy sauce**
4 tablespoons	**miso**
$1/2$ teaspoon	**sesame oil**

Heat olive oil in a large saucepan or a wok and cook the ginger, garlic, and pork on medium heat until pork is no longer pink. Add carrots, sprouts, and cabbage and saute for 2 minutes, stirring. Add the water, seasoning packets, sugar, and soy sauce; mix and bring to a boil. Add noodles and allow to simmer for 3 minutes. Turn heat down to low and melt miso in the soup. Add sesame oil and remove from heat. Makes 4–6 servings.

CURRIED CHICKEN SOUP

2	**large carrots,** diced
2	**large celery stalks,** diced
1	**small onion,** chopped
³/₄ cup	**butter or margarine**
³/₄ cup	**flour**
2 packages	**chicken or vegetable ramen,** crushed and with seasoning packets
1 teaspoon	**curry powder**
3 cans (12 ounces each)	**evaporated milk**
2 cups	**water**
2 cups	**chicken broth**
3 cups	**cubed cooked chicken**

In a large saucepan, saute carrots, celery, and onion in butter until tender. Stir in the flour, seasoning packets, and curry until smooth. Gradually add milk. Bring to a boil, stirring regularly until thickened. Gradually add water and broth. Return to a boil and add chicken and noodles. Continue to boil for 3 minutes. Remove from heat and serve. Makes 8–10 servings.

TUNA NOODLE STEW

3 cups	**water**
1 package	**shrimp ramen noodles,** with seasoning packet
1 teaspoon	**vinegar**
$1/2$ teaspoon	**lemon juice**
dash	**hot sauce**
pinch	**dill weed**
2 teaspoons	**dried onion flakes**
1 can (6 ounces)	**tuna,** drained

In a medium saucepan, bring water to a boil over medium heat. Add the seasoning packet, vinegar, lemon juice, hot sauce, dill weed, and onion flakes. Allow to simmer for 3 minutes. Add tuna and noodles and cook another 3 minutes. Makes 2–4 servings.

CHICKEN CHILE RAMEN

3 tablespoons	**peanut oil**
3	**shallots,** sliced
2 teaspoons	**minced garlic**
$^1/_4$ teaspoon	**ground ginger**
1	**carrot,** diced
1	**mild green chile,** diced
6 cups	**water**
2 tablespoons	**soy sauce**
2 packages	**chicken ramen noodles,** with seasoning packets
2	**chicken breasts,** cooked and diced

Heat oil in a large frying pan over medium high heat. Once oil is warm, add shallots and stir. Add the garlic, ginger, carrot, and chile and stir. When the vegetables have softened slightly, add water, soy sauce, and seasoning packets. Mix and allow to simmer for 5–10 minutes. Add noodles and chicken and allow to cook another 3 minutes. Makes 4–6 servings.

SALADS

BROCCOLI SLAW

²/₃ cup	**vegetable oil**
¹/₃ cup	**white vinegar**
¹/₄ cup	**sugar**
1 package	**chicken ramen noodles,** crushed and with seasoning packet
1 package (16 ounces)	**broccoli coleslaw**
2 bunches	**green onions,** thinly sliced
³/₄ cup	**dried cranberries**
¹/₂ cup	**sliced almonds**
¹/₂ cup	**sunflower seeds**

In a small bowl, combine oil, vinegar, sugar, and seasoning packet to make the dressing. Mix until sugar dissolves and chill for at least 30 minutes.

Combine broccoli coleslaw, onions, and cranberries in a large bowl.

In a medium bowl, combine the almonds, noodles, and sunflower seeds. When ready to serve, combine all ingredients together and toss. Makes 6 servings.

ORIENTAL CHICKEN SALAD

³/₄ cup plus 3 tablespoons	**vegetable oil,** divided
4 ½ tablespoons	**seasoned rice vinegar**
4 ½ tablespoons	**sugar**
2 packages	**oriental ramen noodles,** finely crushed and with seasoning packets
I cup	**slivered almonds**
I head	**cabbage,** shredded
I bunch	**green onions,** finely chopped
2 cups	**cooked and diced chicken breasts**
3 tablespoons	**sunflower seeds**

In a small bowl, mix ³/₄ cup oil, vinegar, sugar, and I seasoning packet to make the dressing.

In a medium frying pan, add remaining oil and noodles. Cook over medium heat until lightly brown. Add almonds and continue to cook until almonds are toasted. Remove from pan and set aside.

Combine cabbage, onions, chicken, and sunflower seeds in a large bowl. Add the noodle mixture and toss. Add dressing and toss to coat. Makes 6 servings.

COLE SLAW

1 package	**chicken ramen noodles,** finely crushed and with seasoning packet
1/4 cup	**apple cider vinegar**
1/4 cup	**sugar**
1/2 teaspoon	**salt**
1/4 teaspoon	**black pepper**
3 tablespoons	**canola oil**
2 teaspoons	**sesame oil**
1 package (16 ounces)	**coleslaw mix**
6	**green onions,** thinly sliced
1 cup	**sliced almonds,** toasted
1/2 teaspoon	**celery seed**

In medium bowl, add noodles, seasoning packet, vinegar, sugar, salt, and pepper. Stir to mix well. Add oils and stir well to make the dressing. Allow to sit at least 5 minutes but no more than 10 minutes.

In large bowl, add slaw mix, onions, almonds, and celery seed. Toss to mix. Add noodle dressing and toss to coat. Portion and serve. Makes 8–10 servings.

MANDARIN SALAD

2 packages	**any flavor ramen noodles,** crushed
I cup	**peanuts,** chopped
I package (16 ounces)	**coleslaw mix**
I bunch	**green onions,** sliced
I	**small red bell pepper,** sliced
I can (15 ounces)	**mandarin orange segments,** drained
¹/₂ cup	**sugar**
¹/₂ cup	**vegetable oil**
¹/₄ cup	**cider vinegar**
I tablespoon	**soy sauce**

Preheat oven to 350 degrees.

Place the noodles and peanuts on a baking sheet and toast until golden brown; about 15 minutes. Remove from pan and allow to cool.

In a large bowl, combine coleslaw, onions, bell pepper, oranges, noodles, and peanuts; toss.

In a small bowl, mix the sugar, oil, vinegar, and soy sauce until well combined. Pour over the salad and toss to coat. Makes 6–8 servings.

NUTTY-GRAPE SALAD

I head	**romaine lettuce,** chopped into bite-size pieces
20	**purple grapes,** halved
3	**green onions,** sliced
I ½ cups	**raspberry vinaigrette**
I package	**any flavor ramen noodles,** crushed
½ cup	**chopped walnuts**

Toss together the lettuce, grapes, and onions. Add vinaigrette and toss to coat. Add noodles and walnuts; toss again and serve. Makes 6–8 servings.

QUICK CHICKEN SALAD

2	**boneless chicken breast halves,** cooked and diced
$^1/_2$ cup	**almonds**
2	**green onions,** sliced
I tablespoon	**sugar**
2 tablespoons	**sesame seeds**
I package	**chicken ramen noodles,** crushed and with seasoning packet
$^1/_2$ medium head	**lettuce,** shredded
$^1/_2$ cup	**vegetable oil**
3 tablespoons	**distilled white vinegar**

In a large bowl, combine the chicken, almonds, onions, sugar, sesame seeds, noodles, and lettuce.

In a small bowl, combine the oil, seasoning packet, and vinegar. Pour dressing over salad and toss to coat. Let stand overnight in refrigerator. Makes 6–8 servings.

TANGERINE CHICKEN SALAD

I large can (15 ounces)	**tangerines or mandarin oranges,** juice reserved
1/4 cup	**cider vinegar**
2 tablespoons	**sugar**
2 tablespoons	**soy sauce**
2 teaspoons plus I tablespoon	**sesame oil,** divided
2 packages	**chicken ramen noodles,** crushed
2 tablespoons	**sesame seeds**
1/2 cup	**slivered almonds**
1/2 head	**red or green cabbage,** sliced
I cup	**shredded carrots**
I bunch	**green onions,** chopped
I head	**lettuce,** sliced
I	**chicken breast,** cooked and finely diced

Preheat the oven to 350 degrees.

Whisk together the reserved juice, vinegar, sugar, soy sauce, and 2 teaspoons sesame oil to make the dressing; set aside.

In a medium bowl, toss the noodles, sesame seeds, almonds, and remaining sesame oil. Spread the mixture onto a baking sheet and bake for 10 minutes. Stir and bake 5 minutes more, or until the noodles are golden brown. Allow to cool completely.

In a large serving bowl, combine the cabbage, carrots, onions, and lettuce. Add the toasted noodle mixture, tangerines, chicken, and dressing; toss to coat. Makes 6–8 servings.

SPROUTING RAMEN SALAD

6 cups	**water**
2 packages	**any flavor ramen noodles**
$^2/_3$ cup	**alfalfa sprouts**
3 tablespoons	**sesame seeds**
$^1/_4$ cup	**red wine vinegar**
2 tablespoons	**soy sauce**
2 tablespoons	**sesame oil**
1 $^1/_2$ tablespoons	**sugar**
1 teaspoon	**Chinese red chili sauce**
$^1/_3$ cup	**sliced green onions**
2 tablespoons	**minced fresh gingerroot**
2 cups	**bean sprouts**
$^1/_2$ cup	**radish sprouts**

In a large saucepan, bring water to a boil. Add noodles and cook for
3 minutes; drain and set aside. Pull alfalfa sprouts apart; set aside.

In a small ungreased frying pan over high heat, toast the sesame seeds
until golden, about 4 minutes. Remove from pan and set aside.

Combine the vinegar, soy sauce, sesame oil, sugar, chili sauce, onions,
and ginger. Mix well and add to noodles; toss to coat and refrigerate for
at least 1 hour.

Toss noodles with sprouts and seeds. Makes 4–6 servings.

POLISH RAMEN SALAD

3 teaspoons	**mayonnaise**
I cup	**plain yogurt**
2 teaspoons	**paprika**
3 packages	**chicken ramen noodles,** crushed and with seasoning packets
2	**tomatoes,** diced
I	**cucumber,** diced
I can (15 ounces)	**corn,** drained
I can (12.5 ounces)	**kidney beans,** rinsed and drained

In a large bowl, whisk the mayonnaise, yogurt, paprika, and I seasoning packet. Add noodles and toss to coat. Add the tomatoes, cucumber, corn, and beans. Toss to coat and refrigerate for at least I hour. Makes 6–8 servings.

FRUIT SALAD

2	**large oranges,** peeled and diced
l	**large pear,** diced
l	**large apple,** diced
5 tablespoons	**brown sugar**
l package	**any flavor ramen noodles,** crushed

In a large bowl, combine the fruit and brown sugar. Mix well and allow it to sit for 5 minutes; toss. Just before serving, add crushed noodles and toss again. Makes 4–6 servings.

CHICKEN FAJITA RAMEN SALAD

I package	**spicy ramen noodles,** crushed and with seasoning packet
2	**boneless chicken breasts**
3 tablespoons	**vegetable oil,** divided
I	**small onion,** sliced
I	**small red bell pepper,** sliced
I	**small green bell pepper,** sliced
I	**large tomato,** diced
2	**limes,** juiced
I teaspoon	**dried cilantro**
2 tablespoons	**soy sauce**
½ tablespoon	**cayenne pepper**
I teaspoon	**sugar**

Lightly sprinkle seasoning packet on both sides of chicken breasts (using about ¼ of the packet in all). Place 2 tablespoons oil in a large frying pan over medium heat. Brown each side of chicken breasts, then cover and cook until done. Cut into strips and place in a large bowl. Saute the onion and bell peppers in the pan until tender. Add to chicken, along with noodles and tomato; toss to mix.

Whisk together the lime juice, cilantro, soy sauce, cayenne pepper, sugar, remaining oil, and remaining seasoning from packet. Drizzle over chicken mixture and toss. Can be served immediately or chilled and served cold. Makes 6–8 servings.

TOFU SALAD

2 cups	**cubed tofu**
2 tablespoons	**soy sauce**
$1/4$ teaspoon	**garlic powder**
$1/4$ teaspoon	**onion powder**
2 tablespoons	**sugar**
3 tablespoons	**white vinegar**
$1/8$ cup, plus 1 tablespoon	**sesame oil,** divided
$1/8$ cup	**olive oil**
1 package	**any flavor ramen noodles,** crushed
3 tablespoons	**sesame seeds**
$1/4$ cup	**slivered almonds**
4	**green onions,** thinly sliced
1	**red bell pepper,** diced
$1/2$ head	**cabbage,** shredded

Preheat the oven to 350 degrees. Place tofu on several paper towels, cover with another paper towel, and press to remove liquid.

In a small bowl, whisk the soy sauce, garlic powder, onion powder, sugar, vinegar, $1/8$ cup sesame oil, and olive oil. Place in a ziplock bag and add tofu. Flip to distribute marinade. Allow to sit 5 minutes, shaking regularly.

In a small bowl, add crushed noodles, sesame seeds, almonds, and remaining sesame oil; toss to coat. Spread the mixture onto a baking sheet and bake for 10 minutes. Stir and bake 5 minutes more, or until the noodles are golden brown. Allow to cool completely.

In a large bowl, combine the onions, bell pepper, and cabbage. Add toasted mixture and tofu with marinade; toss to coat. Makes 4–6 servings.

ORIENTAL SALAD

½ cup	**oil**
¼ cup	**apple cider vinegar**
2 tablespoons	**sugar**
2 packages	**oriental ramen noodles,** crushed with seasoning packets
⅓ cup	**sliced almonds**
¼ cup	**sesame seeds**
2 tablespoons	**butter or margarine,** melted
I head	**green cabbage,** shredded
I	**red bell pepper,** thinly sliced
I	**orange bell pepper,** thinly sliced
I cup	**snow peas**
4	**green onions,** thinly sliced

In a medium bowl, whisk the oil, vinegar, sugar, and I seasoning packet to make dressing; set aside.

In a medium bowl, combine almonds, sesame seeds, noodles, and butter; toss to coat. Transfer to a frying pan and cook over medium heat until almonds are toasted. Do not burn. Remove from pan and set aside.

In a large bowl, combine the cabbage, bell peppers, snow peas, and onions; toss. Just before serving, combine the toasted mixture with the cabbage and toss. Pour the dressing over salad and toss to coat. Makes 8–10 servings.

SIDES

GRILLED RAMEN

I package	**ramen noodles,** chicken, pork, or beef with seasoning packet
2 tablespoons	**soy sauce**
dash	**hot sauce**
dash	**sesame oil**
I tablespoon	**marmalade**
1/4 cup	**hot water,** not boiling

In a ziplock bag, combine the seasoning packet, soy sauce, hot sauce, sesame oil, marmalade, and hot water. Mix thoroughly. Add brick of noodles and seal completely. Tilt bag to allow marinade to coat the entire brick. Allow to sit for at least 15 minutes but no longer than 30 minutes. Flip occasionally to prevent marinade from pooling in one spot.

Over a medium flame, grill noodle brick for 3 minutes each side or until char marks appear. Be sure the brick is not stuck to the grill or it may pull apart when you try to flip or remove it. Serve with remaining marinade as "au jus" or place in a bowl and add I cup of boiling water for a less crunchy dish. Makes 4 servings.

CHINESE FRIED NOODLES

2 cups	**water**
1 package	**oriental ramen noodles,** with seasoning packet
2 tablespoons	**oil**
1 heaping teaspoon	**minced garlic**
1 tablespoon	**soy sauce**
1 teaspoon	**oyster sauce**

In small saucepan, bring water to a boil. Add noodles and cook for 3 minutes, drain and set aside.

In a medium frying pan or wok, heat oil over medium heat. Add garlic, half the seasoning packet, soy sauce, and oyster sauce. Add noodles and fry until noodles begin to crisp, about 3–4 minutes. Makes 1–2 servings.

STUFFED TOMATOES

8	**large tomatoes**
dash	**salt**
I cup	**water**
I package	**chicken or vegetable ramen noodles,** crushed and with seasoning packet
1/2 pound	**sliced fresh mushrooms**
2 tablespoons	**butter or margarine**
I tablespoon	**flour**
1/2 cup	**half-and-half**
2 tablespoons	**breadcrumbs**
I cup	**grated cheddar cheese,** divided

Preheat oven to 400 degrees.

Cut tomatoes in half, scoop out pulp, and set aside. Sprinkle tomatoes with salt and invert on paper towels and let drain, about 15 minutes.

In a small saucepan, bring water to boil, add noodles, and let boil for 2 minutes; drain and set aside.

In a medium frying pan, saute mushrooms in butter for 5 minutes. Add seasoning packet and flour; gradually stir in the half-and-half. Bring to a simmer stirring constantly until thick, about 2 minutes. Remove from heat and stir in breadcrumbs and 1/2 cup cheese. Add noodles and mix. Spoon into tomato cups and sprinkle with remaining cheese. Prepare two 9 x 13-inch baking dishes with nonstick cooking spray. Place tomatoes in dishes and bake, uncovered, for 10 minutes. Makes 16 servings.

TUNA NOODLE SPREAD

I cup	**water**
I package	**beef ramen noodles,** crushed and with seasoning packet
2	**hard-boiled eggs,** chopped
I can (6 ounces)	**tuna,** drained
3 tablespoons	**mayonnaise**
24	**saltine crackers**

In a small saucepan, bring water to a boil. Add noodles and let boil for 2 minutes; drain.

In a medium bowl, combine the seasoning packet, eggs, tuna, and mayonnaise. Add the noodles and thoroughly mix together. If it seems dry, add more mayonnaise. The mixture should be just moist enough to hold together. Serve on saltine crackers. Makes 6–8 servings.

BAKED RAMEN CAKES

1/2 cup	**water**
1 package	**ramen noodles,** any kind, with seasoning packet
1/4 cup	**olive oil**

Preheat oven to 250 degrees.

In a small saucepan, bring water to a low simmer over medium heat. Reduce heat to medium low and add noodles. Cook for 30 seconds, flip and sprinkle with half the seasoning packet. Continue to cook until water is nearly gone. Sprinkle with remaining seasoning. Add olive oil and gently turn noodles in pan until noodles are well covered in oil; drain oil. Use a spoon to remove noodles from pan and place on a baking sheet. Arrange so noodles are in small circular shapes. Bake in oven for 30 minutes or until light brown and crispy. Use on salads, soups, or stir-fry. Makes 8–10 cakes.

SWEET AND SALTY RAMEN

4 cups	**water**
2 packages	**oriental ramen noodles,** with seasoning packets
1 ½ tablespoons	**soy sauce**
2 teaspoons	**brown sugar**
1 tablespoon	**cold butter or margarine**

In a saucepan, bring water to a boil. Add noodles and let boil for 2 minutes; drain and set aside.

In the same pan add the soy sauce, brown sugar, seasoning packets, and a touch of water. Remove from heat and add cold butter. Stir until melted. Add noodles and toss. Serve with chicken or steak. Makes 4–6 servings.

TWISTED RAMEN

4 cups	**water,** divided
2 packages	**any flavor ramen noodles,** with seasoning packets
3	**eggs,** divided
1 ½ cups	**flour**
1 teaspoon	**salt**
4 cups	**vegetable oil**

In a medium saucepan, bring 3 cups water to a boil. Add noodles and let boil for 2 minutes; drain and set aside.

In a medium bowl, make a batter using 1 egg, flour, 1 seasoning packet, and remaining water. Beat remaining eggs in a large bowl. Add noodles, and toss to coat.

In a large frying pan, heat the oil. Separate and twist or braid 4–5 noodles together, dry slightly on paper towels, and then dip noodle twists in batter. Fry till golden brown. Serve with butter or your favorite dip. Makes 10–15 twists.

RAMEN PANCAKES

2 cups	**water**
1 package	**any flavor ramen noodles,** with seasoning packet
1	**medium zucchini,** shredded
2	**scallions,** cut in long narrow strips
1	**medium carrot,** shredded
2	**eggs,** beaten
2 tablespoons	**flour**
2 tablespoons	**vegetable oil,** divided

In a small saucepan, bring water to a boil. Add noodles and let boil for 2 minutes; drain and place in a medium bowl. Stir in the zucchini, scallions, carrot, eggs, flour, and half of the seasoning packet.

Heat 1 tablespoon oil in a large nonstick frying pan over medium-high heat. Using half of the noodle mixture, make 4 pancakes. Fry 2–3 minutes per side. Repeat, using remaining oil. Serve as a side with entrees based on ramen flavor. Makes 8 servings.

CASSEROLES

CHICKEN CASSEROLE

¾ cup	**water**
I can (10.5 ounces)	**cream of mushroom soup,** condensed
I can (10.5 ounces)	**cream of chicken soup,** condensed
3 stalks	**celery,** sliced
I cup	**peas**
I	**carrot,** sliced
3 packages	**chicken ramen noodles,** with seasoning packets
I pound	**chicken,** cooked and chopped
½ cup	**Velveeta cheese,** diced

In a large saucepan, heat water, soups, celery, peas, carrots, and I seasoning packet to boiling. Add noodles and simmer for 3 minutes. Add chicken and cheese, mix, and place in a 9 x 13-inch casserole dish. Heat in microwave on medium for 8–10 minutes. Makes 6–8 servings.

CHICKEN BROCCOLI CASSEROLE

3 tablespoons	**butter or margarine**
I package	**chicken ramen noodles,** crushed
I bag (16 ounces)	**frozen chopped broccoli**
4	**chicken breasts,** cooked and diced
I box	**broccoli and cheese rice mix,** cooked according to package directions
I can (4 ounces)	**sliced mushrooms,** drained
I cup	**sour cream**
I cup	**grated cheddar cheese**
I can (10.5 ounces)	**cream of mushroom soup,** condensed
$^1/_2$ cup	**milk**
I tablespoon	**Worcestershire sauce**
dash	**cayenne**

Preheat oven to 350 degrees. Prepare a 9 x 13-inch glass casserole dish with nonstick cooking spray.

In a medium frying pan, melt the butter over medium heat, add noodles, and stir to coat with butter. Cook, stirring until noodles are lightly browned. Set aside for topping.

In a large microwave-safe bowl, add the broccoli and fill with water until broccoli is completely covered. Microwave on high for 6 minutes; drain. Combine with remaining ingredients in a large bowl, mixing well and pour into the casserole dish. Sprinkle noodles on top of casserole and bake for 18–20 minutes, or until heated through and cheese is melted. Makes 6–8 servings.

RAMEN NOODLE CASSEROLE

1 pound	**ground beef**
2 packages	**beef ramen noodles,** with seasoning packets
1	**medium onion,** chopped
3 cups	**water**
1 can (10.5 ounces)	**cream of mushroom soup,** condensed
1 can (10.5 ounces)	**cream of celery soup,** condensed
1 can (5 ounces)	**sliced water chestnuts**
1/2 cup	**milk**
1 cup	**grated cheddar cheese,** divided

Preheat oven to 350 degrees.

In a large frying pan, brown the ground beef with seasoning packets and onion. In a medium saucepan, bring water to a boil and add the noodles; cook for 3 minutes and then drain. When beef is browned, add noodles, soups, water chestnuts, milk, and 1/2 cup cheese. Pour into an 8 x 8-inch glass baking dish that has been prepared with nonstick cooking spray and top with remaining cheese. Bake uncovered for 20–25 minutes. Makes 4–6 servings.

MEXICAN RAMEN CASSEROLE

1 pound	**ground beef**
2 cups	**chunky salsa,** divided
2 cups	**water**
2 packages	**beef ramen noodles,** with seasoning packets
1 can (15 ounces)	**corn,** drained
1 cup	**grated cheddar cheese**

Preheat oven to 350 degrees.

Brown the ground beef in a large saucepan; drain. Mix in 1 cup of salsa. Add water, noodles, seasoning packets, and corn and bring to a boil and cook, covered, for 3 minutes. Remove cover and simmer until water has evaporated.

Pour into an 8 x 8-inch glass baking dish that has been prepared with nonstick cooking spray and sprinkle cheese on top. Bake for 6–8 minutes, or until cheese is melted. Makes 4–6 servings.

CHEESY TURKEY CASSEROLE

2 cups	**water**
I package	**oriental ramen noodles,** with seasoning packet
$^1/_4$ cup	**frozen mixed vegetables**
$^1/_4$ cup	**diced turkey**
$^1/_4$ cup	**Mexican cheese blend**
4 slices	**Swiss cheese,** diced
4 tablespoons	**Italian-style breadcrumbs**

Preheat oven to 400 degrees. Prepare an 8 x 8-inch casserole dish with nonstick cooking spray.

In a medium saucepan, bring water to a boil. Add the noodles and vegetables and cook for 3 minutes; drain. Add the seasoning packet, turkey, and Mexican cheese blend.

Pour half of the mixture into the casserole dish. Top with half the Swiss cheese. Add remaining mixture, top with remaining Swiss cheese and sprinkle with the breadcrumbs. Bake for 8–10 minutes or until crust has browned. Makes I–2 servings.

LAYERED RAMEN

I pound	**ground beef**
I	**small onion,** diced
2 packages	**chicken ramen noodles,** with seasoning packets
I cup	**grated mozzarella cheese,** divided
I cup	**grated cheddar cheese,** divided
3	**eggs**
2 cups	**water**
I cup	**spaghetti sauce**

Preheat oven to 325 degrees.

In large frying pan, brown the beef, onion, and I seasoning packet. Drain and pour into an 8 x 8-inch casserole dish that has been prepared with nonstick cooking spray. Sprinkle $^1/_4$ cup of each cheese over the beef.

Beat the eggs and cook in the same pan as the beef. Place the egg evenly over the beef and sprinkle another $^1/_4$ cup of each cheese over top.

In a small saucepan bring water to a boil. Add noodles and cook for 3 minutes; drain. Mix the spaghetti sauce into the noodles and pour on top of the eggs. Sprinkle the remaining cheese over the noodles. Bake for 10 minutes, or until cheese is melted. Makes 4–6 servings.

BROCCOLI AND HAM CASSEROLE

4 cups	**water**
2 packages	**chicken ramen noodles,** with seasoning packets
2 large heads	**broccoli,** cut into bite-size pieces
2 cups	**plain yogurt**
4	**eggs**
I package (12 ounces)	**mushrooms,** washed and sliced
2 cups	**cooked diced ham**
2 cups	**grated mild cheddar cheese**
I	**medium onion,** diced

Preheat oven to 350 degrees. Prepare a 12 x 17-inch casserole dish with nonstick cooking spray.

In a medium saucepan, bring water to a boil. Add noodles and cook for 3 minutes; drain.

In a large microwave-safe bowl, add the broccoli and fill with water until broccoli is completely covered. Microwave on high for 6 minutes; drain.

In a large bowl, combine the yogurt, eggs, and seasoning packets; mix thoroughly. Add the broccoli, mushrooms, ham, cheese, onion, and noodles then toss together to evenly coat. Pour into prepared dish and bake for I hour, or until center is bubbly. Allow to set for 15 minutes before serving. Makes 6–8 servings.

TUNA RAMEN CASSEROLE

½ cup	**butter or margarine,** divided
1 cup	**onion,** diced and divided
1½ cups	**stuffing mix**
1 cup	**milk**
1 cup	**chicken broth**
1 tablespoon	**dry mustard**
2 packages	**any flavor ramen noodles,** with seasoning packets
1 cup	**grated cheddar cheese**
4 slices	**American cheese**
2 cans (6 ounces each)	**tuna,** drained and flaked

Preheat oven to 375 degrees.

Add 6 tablespoons butter to a large frying pan. Over low heat, melt the butter and saute ¾ cup onion. Cook for about 5 minutes, or until onion becomes translucent. Add stuffing to pan and toss to coat; set aside.

Combine the milk, broth, remaining butter, dry mustard, and seasoning packets in a medium saucepan and heat over low heat until hot, not boiling. Add the cheeses and remaining onion. Continue to cook on low heat until cheese melts. Break noodle packages in half and add to milk and broth mixture. Cook noodles until they separate easily. Add tuna and mix well. Pour tuna noodle mixture into a 9 x 13-inch casserole dish that has been prepared with nonstick cooking spray and sprinkle stuffing mixture over top. Bake for 30 minutes. Makes 4–6 servings.

TOMATO-BASIL TURKEY CASSEROLE

4 cups	**water**
2 packages	**any flavor ramen noodles**
2 cups	**diced cooked turkey**
I jar (26 ounces)	**pasta sauce**
I	**medium zucchini,** cut in half lengthwise, then cut into slices
I can (2.25 ounces)	**sliced ripe olives,** drained
I teaspoon	**dried basil leaves**
$1/4$ cup	**grated fresh Parmesan cheese**

Preheat oven to 375 degrees. Prepare a 2-quart casserole dish with nonstick cooking spray.

In a medium saucepan, bring water to a boil. Add noodles and cook for 3 minutes; drain. Add the turkey, pasta sauce, zucchini, olives, and basil; mix thoroughly. Add to casserole dish and cover. Bake for 30 minutes. Sprinkle with cheese. Bake, uncovered, for 15–20 minutes more, or until bubbly and thoroughly heated. Makes 6–8 servings.

VEGETABLE

BOK CHOY RAMEN

1/4 cup	**vegetable oil**
1 package	**any flavor ramen noodles,** crushed
1/3 cup	**olive oil**
1/2 cup	**sugar**
1 teaspoon	**soy sauce**
1/4 cup	**vinegar**
1 head	**bok choy,** thinly sliced
1/4 cup	**sliced green onion**
1/2 cup	**sliced almonds**

Heat oil in a large frying pan. Add noodles and fry until lightly brown, stirring constantly.

In a small saucepan, combine olive oil, sugar, soy sauce, and vinegar to make dressing. Cook over low heat for 2 minutes. Place bok choy and noodles in a bowl and drizzle with dressing. Toss to coat and serve. Makes 1–2 servings.

SPINACH PARMESAN RAMEN

4½ cups	**water,** divided
2 packages	**vegetable ramen noodles,** with seasoning packets
¼ cup	**chopped onion**
I teaspoon	**minced garlic**
¼ cup	**frozen spinach,** thawed and drained
4 tablespoons	**milk**
I tablespoon	**cream cheese**
¼ cup	**grated Parmesan cheese**
¼ cup	**grated mozzarella cheese**

In a large saucepan, bring 4 cups water to a boil. Add noodles and cook 3 minutes; drain and set aside.

In a large saucepan, add remaining water and I seasoning packet, stirring until dissolved. Bring to a boil over medium heat. Add onion and garlic and let simmer for 5 minutes. Stir in spinach and cook for 2 minutes more. Add milk and cheeses, stirring until cheese is melted. Add noodles and toss until coated. Makes 3–4 servings.

ASIAN NOODLE TOSS

2 cups	**water**
I package	**vegetable ramen noodles**
4	**baby carrots,** julienned
¹/₂ cup	**sugar snap peas**
I can (4 ounces)	**mandarin oranges**
I tablespoon	**soy sauce**
I tablespoon	**orange jelly**
I tablespoon	**cider vinegar**

In a small saucepan, bring water to a boil. Add noodles, carrots, and peas and cook for 3 minutes: drain and place in a bowl. Add the oranges, reserving the juice in a small bowl. To the juice, add the soy sauce, jelly, and vinegar; mix thoroughly. Drizzle over noodles, toss and serve warm. Makes I–2 servings.

BROCCOLI AND RAMEN NOODLES

2 cups	**water**
1 package	**vegetable ramen noodles,** with seasoning packet
1 tablespoon	**corn oil**
4 cups	**broccoli**
1/4 cup	**lemon juice**
1/4 cup	**honey**
1/2 teaspoon	**pepper**
1 cup	**unsalted peanuts,** chopped

In a small saucepan, bring water to a boil. Add noodles and cook
3 minutes; drain and toss in oil. Place broccoli in a microwave-save
bowl and add enough water to cover. Microwave on high for 4 minutes;
drain well and add noodles.

In a small bowl, combine the lemon juice, honey, pepper, and
seasoning packet; mix thoroughly. Drizzle over broccoli and noodles.
Top with peanuts and toss to coat. Serve warm. Makes 2–4 servings.

YAKISOBA

6 cups	**water**
4 packages	**any flavor ramen noodles**
1/2 teaspoon	**sesame oil**
1 tablespoon	**canola oil**
2 tablespoons	**chile paste**
2 cloves	**garlic,** chopped
1/2 cup	**soy sauce,** divided
1	**onion,** sliced lengthwise into eighths
1/2 medium head	**cabbage,** coarsely chopped
2	**carrots,** coarsely chopped

In a large saucepan, bring water to a boil. Add noodles and cook 3 minutes; drain and set aside.

In a large frying pan, combine the oils and chile paste and then stir-fry for 30 seconds. Add the garlic and 1/4 cup soy sauce and stir-fry 30 seconds more. Add the onion, cabbage, and carrots. Stir-fry until cabbage begins to wilt. Stir in remaining soy sauce and cooked noodles. Continue to cook until noodles barely begin to crisp. Makes 4–6 servings.

PAD THAI

2 packages	**vegetable ramen noodles,** with seasoning packets
3 tablespoons	**soy sauce**
2 tablespoons	**sesame oil**
1 package (16 ounces)	**extra firm tofu,** cubed
4 cups	**water**
1 bag (32 ounces)	**frozen stir-fry vegetables**
	peanut sauce

In a small bowl, combine 1 seasoning packet, soy sauce, and sesame oil. Transfer to a ziplock bag and add tofu. Seal and toss to coat. Allow to marinate for 1–2 hours.

In a medium saucepan, bring water to a boil. Add noodles and cook 3 minutes; drain and set aside.

Remove tofu from marinade and pour remaining marinade into a large frying pan or wok. Add vegetables and cook over medium heat until vegetables become soft. Add tofu and continue to cook, stirring gently, until tofu is heated. Add noodles and allow them to cook until they absorb most of the remaining liquid in the pan. Transfer to a bowl and toss with peanut sauce. Makes 2–4 servings.

OHM RAISU RAMEN

2 cups	**water**
I package	**vegetable ramen noodles,** with seasoning packet
3	**eggs**
2 cups	**cooked rice**
¼ cup	**bean sprouts**
I can (5 ounces)	**sliced water chestnuts,** drained

In a small saucepan, bring water to a boil. Add noodles with seasoning packet and cook 2 minutes.

Fry the eggs, breaking the yolks and cooking until eggs have completely solidified; set aside. Put rice into bottom of a large microwave-safe bowl and then add noodles with broth. Slice the eggs into thin strips and add to noodles. Add the bean sprouts and water chestnuts. Place in microwave and cook on high for I minute. Makes 1–2 servings.

OLIVE AND RED PEPPER RAMEN

4 cups	**water**
2 packages	**any flavor ramen noodles**
1	**medium red bell pepper,** chopped
3/4 cup	**sliced fresh mushrooms**
1/2 cup	**chopped onion**
1 1/2 teaspoons	**minced garlic**
1 tablespoon	**vegetable oil**
15	**stuffed green olives,** sliced

In a medium saucepan, bring water to a boil. Add noodles and cook for 3 minutes; drain and set aside.

In a large frying pan, saute the bell pepper, mushrooms, onion, and garlic in oil, until softened. Add olives and noodles; toss and serve. Makes 4–6 servings.

SPICY LIME RAMEN

2 cups	**water**
I package	**chili ramen noodles,** with seasoning packet
pinch	**garlic powder**
pinch	**cayenne pepper**
I	**green onion,** sliced
1/2 teaspoon	**finely chopped cilantro**
1/2	**lime,** juiced

In a small saucepan, bring water to a boil. Add noodles and cook for 3 minutes; drain and reserve 1/4 cup of the water.

In a small bowl, mix seasoning packet, garlic, and cayenne; add to reserved water and mix until seasonings have dissolved. Add to noodles and toss to coat. Top with onion, cilantro, and lime juice, to taste. Makes I–2 servings.

ITALIAN RAMEN PATTIES

8 cups	**water**
4 packages	**any flavor ramen noodles**
2 teaspoons	**olive oil,** divided
4	**medium carrots,** cut into thin strips
1 teaspoon	**dried basil leaves**
1/4 teaspoon	**salt**
1 package (10 ounces)	**frozen chopped spinach,** thawed and drained
2	**eggs,** slightly beaten
1/2 cup	**ricotta cheese**
1/4 cup	**grated Parmesan cheese**
1/4 teaspoon	**pepper**
2 cups	**spaghetti sauce,** warmed

In a large saucepan, bring water to a boil. Add noodles and cook for 2 minutes; drain and set aside.

Heat 1 teaspoon oil in a large frying pan over medium heat. Cook carrots, basil, salt, and spinach for 2 minutes, stirring occasionally, until carrots are tender-crisp.

In a large bowl, mix the noodles, eggs, cheeses, and pepper. Shape pasta mixture into 4 patties, each about 1-inch thick.

Heat remaining oil in a large frying pan over medium-high heat. Cook patties for 6–8 minutes, turning after 4 minutes, until golden brown. Top patties with vegetable mixture and spaghetti sauce. Makes 4 servings.

MUSHROOM AND ZUCCHINI RAMEN

6 cups	**water**
3 packages	**vegetable ramen noodles,** with seasoning packets
2 medium	**zucchini,** thinly sliced
1/2 pound	**fresh mushrooms,** sliced
2	**green onions,** chopped
1 tablespoon	**minced garlic**
2 tablespoons	**butter or margarine**
1 tablespoon	**olive oil**
1	**large tomato,** diced
2 teaspoons	**minced fresh basil**
1 cup	**grated provolone cheese**
3 tablespoons	**grated Parmesan cheese**

In a medium saucepan, bring water to a boil. Add noodles and cook for 3 minutes; drain and set aside.

In a large frying pan over medium heat, saute the zucchini, mushrooms, onions, and garlic in butter and oil for 4 minutes. Add the tomato, basil, and 2 seasoning packets and stir. Cover and simmer for 3 minutes. Add the noodles and cheese. Toss to coat and serve. Makes 6 servings.

POULTRY

HERBED CHICKEN

4	**chicken breasts,** cut into strips
1 tablespoon	**butter or margarine**
1/2 cup	**diced carrots**
1/4 cup	**diced onion**
2 cups	**water**
2 packages	**chicken ramen noodles,** lightly crushed, with seasoning packets
dash	**dried marjoram**
dash	**dried thyme**
pinch	**dried rosemary**
pinch	**rubbed sage**

In a large frying pan, saute the chicken in butter over medium heat until lightly brown. Add the carrots and onion; saute until tender. Add water, 1 seasoning packet, and spices. Increase the heat and bring to a boil. Add noodles and continue to boil until water evaporates, stirring often. Makes 4–5 servings.

GARLIC CHICKEN TOSS

5	**green onions,** chopped
2 tablespoons	**minced garlic**
2 tablespoons	**butter or margarine**
2 tablespoons	**olive oil**
4	**chicken breasts,** diced
3 tablespoons	**lemon juice**
3 tablespoons	**fresh parsley**
2 packages	**chicken ramen noodles,** with seasoning packets
4 cups	**water**

In a large frying pan, saute the onions and garlic in butter and oil until tender. Stir in the chicken, lemon juice, parsley, and 1 seasoning packet. Saute until chicken is golden brown.

In a medium saucepan, bring water to a boil. Add noodles and cook for 3 minutes; drain. Add chicken mixture and toss. Makes 4–5 servings.

THAI CHICKEN

4 cups	**water**
2 packages	**chicken ramen noodles,** with seasoning packets
1/2 cup	**shredded cooked chicken**
1	**carrot,** thinly sliced with a vegetable peeler
1/2	**cucumber,** peeled, seeds removed, and thinly sliced
4 tablespoons	**spicy Thai peanut sauce**

In a medium saucepan, bring water and 1 seasoning packet to a boil. Add noodles and cook for 3 minutes; drain. Toss noodles with remaining ingredients, adding more peanut sauce if needed until evenly coated, but not runny. Chill slightly or serve at room temperature. Makes 3–4 servings.

CAESAR CHICKEN RAMEN

4 cups	**water**
2 packages	**any flavor ramen noodles**
1/2 cup	**Caesar salad dressing**
2	**boneless, skinless chicken breasts,** cooked and diced
1/2 cup	**croutons**
1/4 cup	**cooked and crumbled bacon**

In a medium saucepan, bring water to a boil. Add noodles and cook for 2 minutes; drain. Add dressing and toss to coat. Allow to chill in refrigerator for 1 hour. Add remaining ingredients and toss. Makes 2–4 servings.

HONEY GRILLED CHICKEN

I tablespoon	**creamy peanut butter**
1/2 teaspoon	**red pepper flakes**
1/4 teaspoon	**ground ginger**
I teaspoon	**garlic powder**
1/4 cup	**honey**
1/3 cup	**rice vinegar**
2 tablespoons	**soy sauce**
I tablespoon	**sesame oil**
2 tablespoons	**vegetable oil**
3	**boneless, skinless chicken breasts**
3 cups	**water**
2	**medium carrots,** sliced
2 cups	**broccoli florets**
I	**medium red bell pepper,** sliced
I package	**any flavor ramen noodles**
2	**green onions,** thinly sliced

Preheat the grill. In a medium bowl, combine peanut butter, red pepper flakes, ginger, garlic, honey, rice vinegar, soy sauce, and oils; stir to blend. Put 4 tablespoons of sauce in a ziplock bag for marinating; set aside remaining sauce. Place chicken in marinade in bag; seal and shake to coat. Refrigerate for at least 30 minutes or overnight.

In a large saucepan, bring water to a boil. Add carrots, broccoli, and bell pepper and cook over high heat until water comes to a rolling boil. Reduce heat to medium, add noodles and allow to cook for 3 minutes; drain. In a large bowl, combine the noodles and vegetables with the remaining sauce and onions. Toss to coat and cover with plastic wrap.

Grill chicken breasts over medium-hot coals for about 10 minutes, 5 minutes on each side or until done and juices run clear. Remove from grill and slice. Serve noodles topped with chicken slices. Makes 3–6 servings.

TURKEY-PASTA PIE

¹/₂ pound	**ground turkey**
¹/₄ cup	**finely chopped onion**
I can (14.5 ounces)	**stewed tomatoes,** with liquid
I can (8 ounces)	**tomato sauce**
¹/₂ teaspoon	**Italian seasoning**
6 cups	**water**
3 packages	**any flavor ramen noodles**
2	**eggs,** divided
I tablespoon	**butter or margarine,** melted
I cup	**grated mozzarella cheese**
I cup	**creamy small-curd cottage cheese**
I package (8 ounces)	**frozen spinach,** thawed and drained
¹/₄ cup	**grated Parmesan cheese**

Preheat oven to 350 degrees.

In a large frying pan, cook the turkey and onion over medium heat; drain. Stir in the tomatoes, tomato sauce, and Italian seasoning and bring to a boil; reduce heat. Cover and simmer for 10 minutes, stirring occasionally.

In a large saucepan, bring water to a boil. Add noodles and cook for 2 minutes; drain and set aside. Beat I egg and the butter in a large bowl. Add the noodles and mozzarella cheese; toss to mix. Place mixture into an ungreased 10-inch pie plate and press evenly on bottom and up side.

Mix the cottage cheese and remaining egg and then spread over the noodle mixture. Sprinkle with the spinach. Spoon turkey mixture evenly over top and then sprinkle with Parmesan cheese. Bake, uncovered, for 30 minutes, or until hot in center. Let stand 10 minutes before cutting. Makes 6 servings.

TURKEY GRAVY NOODLES

3 cups	**water,** divided
1 package	**beef ramen noodles,** with seasoning packet
1/4 cup	**sliced green onions**
1/4 cup	**diced green bell pepper**
1/4 cup	**diced carrot**
2 teaspoons	**olive oil**
dash	**pepper**
1 cup	**turkey gravy**
1	**small tomato,** diced

In a small saucepan, bring 2 cups water to a boil. Add noodles and cook for 2 minutes; drain and set aside.

Place the onions, bell pepper, and carrot in a saute pan, add olive oil and toss to coat. Turn heat to medium and allow to cook for 1 minute, stirring regularly. Add the remaining water and pepper. Cook until there is only a little water left in the bottom of the pan, about 5 minutes. Stir in the seasoning packet. Add the turkey gravy and bring to a simmer. Serve noodles topped with the turkey gravy and tomatoes. Makes 1–2 servings.

TURKEY RAMEN

I pound	**ground turkey**
I	**medium onion,** chopped
2 tablespoons	**flour**
2 $\frac{1}{2}$ cups	**water**
2 packages	**beef ramen noodles,** lightly crushed, with seasoning packets
2 cups	**frozen vegetable stir-fry,** thawed

In a large frying pan, cook turkey with the onion. Sprinkle flour over turkey and onion and blend thoroughly. Continue cooking meat mixture for 2–3 minutes. Add the water, noodles, seasoning packets, and vegetables. Cook for 5 minutes, or until noodles are tender. Let sit for 5 minutes or until gravy has thickened. Makes 2–4 servings.

LEFTOVER THANKSGIVING FRIED RAMEN

2 cups	**water**
1 package	**chicken ramen noodles,** with seasoning packet
4 tablespoons	**vegetable oil,** divided
$1/2$ cup	**diced leftover turkey**
$1/2$ cup	**leftover stuffing**
$1/2$ cup	**chicken broth**

In a small saucepan, bring water to a boil. Add noodles and cook for 3 minutes; drain and set aside.

In a large frying pan, add 2 tablespoons oil. Add the turkey and stuffing and cook over medium heat for 2–3 minutes, or until turkey begins to crisp on edges. Remove turkey and stuffing from pan and then add remaining oil. Place noodles in pan and toss to coat. Cook noodles for 1 minute and then stir in seasoning packet. Once the seasoning is mixed in evenly, add the turkey and stuffing. Gradually pour in the chicken broth; mix well. Cook another 30 seconds or until mixture is warmed through. Makes 1–2 servings.

PESTO TURKEY AND PASTA

4 cups	**water**
2 packages	**any flavor ramen noodles**
2 cups	**diced cooked turkey breast**
1/2 cup	**basil pesto**
1/2 cup	**coarsely chopped roasted red bell peppers**
	sliced black olives (optional)

In a medium saucepan, bring water to a boil. Add noodles and cook for 3 minutes; drain. Add the turkey, pesto, and bell peppers to the noodles. Heat over low heat, stirring constantly, until hot. Serve with a garnish of olives, if desired. Makes 2–4 servings.

MEATS

MEATBALLS AND PINEAPPLE RAMEN

4 cups	**water**
2 packages	**beef ramen noodles,** with seasoning packets
1/2 pound	**ground beef**
2 teaspoons	**garlic powder**
1/3 cup	**vegetable oil**
1 can (8 ounces)	**pineapple chunks,** drained
1	**red bell pepper,** sliced

In a large saucepan, bring water to a boil. Add noodles and cook for 3 minutes; drain and set aside.

In a medium bowl, mix the ground beef, seasoning packets, and garlic powder. Form into small meatballs.

In a large frying pan, heat oil over medium heat. Add the meatballs and brown on all sides. Reduce the heat and allow to simmer for 10 minutes. Add pineapple and bell pepper and continue to cook for 5 minutes more. Add noodles to pan; toss and serve. Makes 4–6 servings.

RAMEN ROLLED STEAK

1 ½ pounds	**flank steaks**
1 package	**beef ramen noodles,** crushed, with seasoning packet
	pepper, to taste
1	**egg**
1 tablespoon	**water**
1 tablespoon	**flour**
2 tablespoons	**steak sauce**

Preheat oven to 350 degrees.

Pound 2 long pieces of flank steak on a board. Sprinkle seasoning packet and pepper on both sides of the steaks and rub in.

In separate bowl, beat the egg and water. Whisk in flour until there are no lumps. Spread the mixture on one side of each of the pounded steaks. Sprinkle evenly with the crushed noodles. Roll up and pin with at least 4 toothpicks in each roll.

Place each roll in a mini loaf pan or place rolls in a baking dish that has been prepared with nonstick cooking spray. Bake for 30–35 minutes, uncovered. Rub rolled steak with steak sauce. Bake for 10 minutes more. Let cool for about 10 minutes before cutting. Slice between toothpicks and serve. Makes 6–8 servings.

YATSOBI

I pound	**lean ground beef**
6 slices	**bacon**
I	**medium red onion,** diced
3 tablespoons	**minced garlic**
3 tablespoons	**soy sauce**
3	**carrots,** cut into thin strips
I	**medium cabbage,** chopped
I	**red bell pepper,** diced
4 cups	**water**
2 packages	**any flavor ramen noodles**
splash	**olive oil**
3 cups	**bean sprouts**

In a large frying pan, brown the ground beef; drain and set aside.

In the same pan, fry the bacon until crispy; drain on paper towels and reserve 2 tablespoons of the bacon fat. Stir the onion and garlic into the fat and cook for 3–4 minutes or until onions are soft. Add the soy sauce and carrots and cook for 2–3 minutes. Add cabbage and bell pepper and stir-fry on medium heat for 5–6 minutes, or until vegetables are tender-crisp. Add ground beef and bacon to the vegetable mixture and cook on medium heat for 2–3 minutes, or until meat is heated through.

In a large saucepan, bring water to a boil. Add noodles and cook for 3 minutes; drain and toss with olive oil to keep from sticking together. Add to meat and vegetable mixture with bean sprouts and cook for 3 minutes, stirring frequently. Makes 4–6 servings.

CROCK-POT BEEF AND NOODLES

2 pounds	**beef roast**
14 cups	**water,** divided
6 packages	**beef ramen noodles,** with seasoning packets
2	**large white onions,** diced

Place roast in a 4-quart crock-pot with 1 cup water on low heat and allow to cook overnight or for 8–9 hours. Shred the meat and add all seasoning packets, onion, and 1 cup water. Allow to cook, on low, another 1–2 hours.

About 15 minutes before serving, bring remaining water to a boil in a large saucepan. Add noodles and cook for 3 minutes. Drain, place in a large serving bowl, and mix in the beef. Makes 10–14 servings.

STUFFED BELL PEPPERS

3	**green bell peppers**
I can (14.5 ounces)	**diced tomatoes,** divided
I can (8 ounces)	**tomato sauce,** divided
I tablespoon	**olive oil**
I	**small onion,** diced
4 tablespoons	**minced garlic**
I pound	**ground beef**
I package	**beef ramen noodles,** finely crushed, and with seasoning packet
¹/₂ cup	**grated Monterey Jack cheese**

Preheat oven to 375 degrees.

Cut bell peppers in half, crosswise. Remove seeds and place on paper towels to drain.

In a medium mixing bowl, combine a third of the tomatoes and half the tomato sauce and set aside.

Add the olive oil to a large frying pan. Heat on medium low and add the onion and garlic. Saute for 4–5 minutes or until soft. Add the beef and seasoning packet, mix well, and continue to cook until beef has browned. Remove from heat. Add the noodles, remaining tomatoes, and remaining tomato sauce; mix well.

Place the bell peppers as bowls in a 9 x 13-inch glass casserole dish and fill with beef mixture. Top with the tomato sauce mixture. Cover with foil and bake for about I hour, or until peppers are tender. Uncover and bake I0 minutes more. Sprinkle with cheese and bake for 5 minutes. Makes 6 servings.

GINGERED PORK AND RAMEN

I pound	**boneless pork shoulder,** cut into 1-inch pieces
2 packages	**chicken ramen noodles,** crumbled and with seasoning packets
I teaspoon	**grated gingerroot**
3 cups	**water**
I cup	**halved fresh snow pea pods**
1/4 cup	**sliced green onion**
I tablespoon	**soy sauce**
2 teaspoons	**cornstarch**

In 3 1/2- to 4-quart crock-pot, combine the pork, seasoning packets, gingerroot and water; mix. Cover and cook on low heat for 6–8 hours.

About 30 minutes before serving, add the noodles, pea pods, and onion; mix. Turn heat setting to high; cover and cook for 10 minutes more or just until vegetables are tender-crisp.

In a small bowl, blend the soy sauce and cornstarch until smooth. Stir into pork mixture and cook for 5 minutes or until sauce is slightly thickened. Makes 4–6 servings.

ORIENTAL HOT DOGS

4 cups	**water**
2 packages	**oriental ramen noodles,** with seasoning packets
1/4 cup	**sliced yellow onion**
1	**zucchini,** diagonally sliced
2	**hot dogs,** diagonally sliced
1/4 cup	**mustard greens**
	chives, to taste

In a large saucepan, bring water to a boil. Add the seasoning packets, onion, and zucchini and reduce to medium heat. Allow to simmer for 1 minute. Add hot dogs and simmer for 1 minute. Add noodles and simmer for 2 minutes. Add mustard greens and simmer for 1 minute more. Serve topped with chives. Makes 1–2 servings.

SPICY SAUSAGE RAMEN

2 to 3	**spicy Italian sausage links**
¼ cup	**diced onion**
½ cup	**diced green bell pepper**
I tablespoon	**minced garlic**
2 cups	**water**
I package	**chili ramen noodles,** with seasoning packet
I can (14.5 ounces)	**stewed tomatoes**

Poke each sausage with a fork to allow grease to escape.

In a large frying pan, cook the sausage over medium heat. Remove sausage and then slice and set aside. Saute the onion, bell pepper, and garlic in the pan with the grease from the sausage.

In a large saucepan, combine water, flavor packet, and tomatoes. Bring to a boil and add noodles, sausage, and vegetables. Cook for 3 minutes. Makes 1–2 servings.

HOT AND SOUR RAMEN

2 1/2 cups	**water,** divided
1 package	**oriental ramen noodles,** lightly crushed, and with seasoning packet
1/2 teaspoon	**lemon juice**
1	**chicken breast,** cooked and diced
1/4 cup	**frozen peas**
1/4 cup	**frozen corn**
1 teaspoon	**hot oil or Mongolian Fire Oil**
1 tablespoon	**soy sauce**
1 tablespoon	**cornstarch**
2	**eggs,** beaten

In a large saucepan bring 2 cups of water to a boil. Add seasoning packet, lemon juice, chicken, peas, corn, hot oil, and soy sauce and cook for 3 minutes. Add noodles and continue to cook for 3 minutes more.

Mix cornstarch in remaining water. Slowly add to pan while stirring constantly. Let cook another minute or until mixture thickens. Slowly add the eggs, stirring constantly. Makes 1–2 servings.

PORK SKILLET

1 tablespoon	**vegetable oil**
³/₄ pound	**pork tenderloin,** cut into strips
2 cups	**water**
1	**medium red bell pepper,** cut into strips
1 cup	**chopped broccoli**
3	**medium green onions,** sliced
2 teaspoons	**parsley flakes**
1 tablespoon	**soy sauce**
2 packages	**pork ramen noodles,** with seasoning packets

In a large frying pan or wok over medium-high heat, add the oil, coating the entire surface.

Add pork and fry about 5 minutes or until no longer pink. Add the water, bell pepper, broccoli, onions, parsley, soy sauce, and seasoning packets. Bring to a boil and then add noodles. Boil for 3 minutes, stirring occasionally, until noodles are completely softened. Makes 3–4 servings.

PEPPERONI PIZZA

8 cups	**water**
4 packages	**beef ramen noodles,** with seasoning packets
I tablespoon	**olive oil**
6 teaspoons	**minced garlic**
I teaspoon	**red pepper flakes**
$^1/_2$ cup	**grated fresh Parmesan cheese**
$^1/_2$ teaspoon	**oregano**
4	**eggs**
$^1/_2$ cup	**cream**
I cup	**ricotta cheese**
	salt and pepper, to taste
2 cups	**grated fontina cheese**
I package (3.5 ounces)	**pepperoni slices**

Preheat oven to 425 degrees. In a large saucepan, bring water to a boil. Add noodles and cook for 3 minutes; drain and set aside. Using a large saucepan, heat olive oil and add the garlic and red pepper flakes, cook and stir for I minute. Remove from heat and add the noodles, Parmesan, and oregano. Toss and transfer noodles to a 10.25-inch deep-dish pizza pan that has been prepared with nonstick cooking spray. Spread noodles out evenly to create the crust of the pizza.

Whisk the eggs with the cream and 2 seasoning packets; pour evenly over the noodles. Bake for 5 minutes, or until eggs have set. Meanwhile, season the ricotta with salt and pepper. Remove pan from oven and spread ricotta evenly over the noodles. Sprinkle the fontina cheese on top of the ricotta and top with pepperoni. Return the pan to the oven and increase the temperature to broil. Cook for 5 minutes, or until the cheese has melted and just begins to brown. Cut pizza into wedges and serve. Makes 6 servings.

SEAFOOD

GARLIC SHRIMP RAMEN

$^1\!/_4$ pound	**pre-cooked shrimp**
3 tablespoons	**butter or margarine**
3 tablespoons	**minced garlic**
1 package	**shrimp ramen noodles,** with seasoning packet
2 cups	**water**

In a medium frying pan, saute shrimp in butter and garlic for 2–3 minutes, adding seasoning packet to taste.

In small saucepan, bring water to a boil. Add noodles and cook for 3 minutes; drain and add to shrimp mixture. Toss and serve. Makes 1–2 servings.

CRAB LO MEIN

5 1/4 cups	**water,** divided
2 packages	**chicken ramen noodles,** with seasoning packets
1	**medium onion,** julienned
1	**medium green bell pepper,** julienned
2 cups	**frozen broccoli cuts,** thawed
1/4 cup	**sliced fresh mushrooms**
2 tablespoons	**canola oil**
1 tablespoon	**cornstarch**
1/4 cup	**soy sauce**
1 can (12 ounces)	**crab meat,** lightly chopped

In a medium saucepan, bring 4 cups water to a boil. Add noodles and cook for 3 minutes; drain and set aside.

In a large frying pan over medium heat, saute the onion, bell pepper, broccoli, and mushrooms in oil for 3–4 minutes or until tender-crisp.

In a small bowl, combine the cornstarch, remaining water, seasoning packets, and soy sauce. Gradually add to pan and cook over medium heat until thick, stirring constantly. Add crab and continue to cook for 2 minutes more. Add to the noodles and then toss and serve. Makes 4–6 servings.

SMOKED MUSSEL RAMEN

4 cups	**water**
2 packages	**chicken ramen noodles,** with seasoning packets
3 tablespoons	**cooking oil**
I can (6.5 ounces)	**mushrooms,** drained
I can (6.5 ounces)	**smoked mussels,** drained
I tablespoon	**garlic powder**
I tablespoon	**onion powder**

In a medium saucepan, bring water to a boil. Add noodles and cook for 3 minutes; drain, add the seasoning packets, stir, and set aside.

In a large frying pan or wok over medium heat, warm the oil. Add the mushrooms, mussels, garlic powder, and onion powder. Cook for 4 minutes, stirring often. Add noodles, lower heat slightly, stir, and then cook for 5 minutes more. Keep stirring until mushrooms and mussels are well blended with the noodles. Makes 2–4 servings.

TERIYAKI TUNA RAMEN

2 cups	**water**
I package	**any flavor ramen noodles**
I can (6 ounces)	**tuna,** drained
I	**carrot,** thinly sliced
$1/4$ teaspoon	**freshly chopped ginger**
$1/4$ teaspoon	**honey**
I tablespoon	**teriyaki sauce**
I	**green onion,** thinly sliced

In a small saucepan, bring water to a boil. Add noodles and cook for 3 minutes; drain, add tuna, and set aside.

In a small saucepan, steam the carrot with the ginger and honey in enough water to barely cover carrots. Cook until tender-crisp, or about 2–3 minutes. Drain and add to tuna and noodles. Top with teriyaki sauce and toss. Serve garnished with onion. Makes 2–4 servings.

SALMON RAMEN

1 can (14.5 ounces)	**diced tomatoes,** with liquid
2 cans (5 ounces each)	**salmon,** drained
2 tablespoons	**olive oil**
2 packages	**vegetable ramen noodles,** with seasoning packets
2 tablespoons	**oregano**
2 tablespoons	**minced garlic**
1 cup	**water**
2 tablespoons	**grated Parmesan cheese**

In a medium saucepan, combine the tomatoes, salmon, olive oil, seasoning packets, oregano, and garlic and bring to a simmer. Add the noodles and water. Cover and cook for 3 minutes. Serve sprinkled with Parmesan cheese. Makes 2–4 servings.

SWEDISH RAMEN

4 cups	**water**
2 packages	**any flavor ramen noodles**
1 can (7 ounces)	**smoked Baltic herring in tomato sauce**

In a small saucepan, bring water to a boil. Add noodles and cook for 3 minutes. Drain, add herring, and toss to coat. Makes 3–4 servings.

CAJUN SEAFOOD NOODLES

2 cups	**water**
pinch	**sugar**
I teaspoon	**butter or margarine**
¹⁄₄ teaspoon	**celery salt**
I teaspoon	**minced garlic**
2 packages	**shrimp ramen noodles,** with seasoning packets
I can (4 ounces)	**cooked shrimp,** drained
I	**chicken breast,** cooked and cubed
¹⁄₄ cup	**cooked and cubed Cajun sausage**

In a medium saucepan, bring the water, sugar, butter, celery salt, garlic, and seasoning packets to a boil. Add the noodles, shrimp, chicken, and sausage. Cook for 3 minutes. Makes 4–6 servings.

RAMEN CLAM CHOWDER PIE

2 cups	**water**
1 package	**any flavor ramen noodles**
1 can (10.75 ounces)	**New England-style clam chowder**
1 (9-inch)	**pre-cooked piecrust**
1/4 cup	**grated cheddar cheese**
10	**Ritz crackers,** crushed

Preheat oven to 350 degrees.

In a small saucepan, bring water to a boil. Add noodles and cook for 3 minutes; drain. Add clam chowder and toss. Pour into pie crust and top with cheese and crackers. Bake for 15 minutes, or until crackers are visibly toasted. Makes 6–8 servings.

SPINACH CRAB RAMEN

2 cups	**water**
2 packages	**vegetable ramen noodles,** with seasoning packets
I package (12 ounces)	**imitation crabmeat**
I can (14 ounces)	**spinach,** drained

In a medium saucepan, bring water to a boil. Add noodles with seasoning packets, crab, and spinach. Cook for 3 minutes. Makes 2–4 servings.

COCONUT CURRY SHRIMP

4 cups	**water**
2 packages	**any flavor ramen noodles**
$1/2$ cup	**coconut milk**
$1/3$ cup	**creamy peanut butter**
1 $1/2$ teaspoon	**curry**
1	**lime,** juiced
1 pound	**large shrimp,** cooked and cleaned
$1/2$	**seedless cucumber,** julienned
4	**scallions,** sliced

Bring water to a boil in a large frying pan. Add noodles and cover. Remove from heat and let stand 5 minutes.

Whisk the coconut milk, peanut butter, curry, and lime juice in a medium bowl to blend. Drain noodles and add shrimp, cucumber, scallions, and coconut milk mixture; toss to coat. Serve at room temperature. Makes 2–4 servings.

DESSERT

CHOCOLATE CHERRY CAKES

¹/₃ cup	**vegetable oil**
1 package	**any flavor ramen noodles,** finely crushed
3	**chocolate cupcakes**
1 cup	**fresh cherries**
¹/₂ cup	**chocolate fudge,** warmed

Heat oil in a large frying pan. Add noodles and fry until lightly brown, stirring constantly; place on paper towels to drain off excess oil.

Break up cake into bite-size pieces. Evenly distribute into 4 serving dishes. Top with cherries and hot fudge. Sprinkle with fried noodles and serve. Makes 4 servings.

CHOCOLATE RAMEN BALLS

4 (1.55 ounces each)	**Nestle Crunch candy bars**
2 tablespoons	**milk**
I tablespoon	**honey**
I package	**any flavor ramen noodles,** finely crushed

In a microwave-safe bowl, combine the candy bars, milk, and honey. Microwave on half power for I minute. Stir and repeat until chocolate is melted. Add noodles and mix until thoroughly coated. Spoon tablespoon-size balls onto wax paper. Allow to cool and serve.
Makes 12 balls

JIGGLY RAMEN

1/3 cup	**vegetable oil**
1 package	**any flavor ramen noodles,** crushed
2 cups	**cold water,** divided
1 package (6 ounces)	**any flavor gelatin**

Heat oil in a large frying pan. Add noodles and fry until lightly brown, stirring constantly; place on a paper towels to drain off excess oil.

Bring 1 cup water to a boil in a small saucepan. Add gelatin and stir until completely dissolved. Add remaining water and noodles, stir and transfer to a gelatin mold. Refrigerate for 4 hours or until set. Unmold before serving. Makes 4–6 servings.

QUICK AND EASY
FRIED ICE CREAM

1/3 cup	**vegetable oil**
1 package	**any flavor ramen noodles,** crushed
1/4 cup	**brown sugar**
1/4 cup	**chocolate sprinkles**
4 scoops	**vanilla ice cream**

Heat oil in a large frying pan. Add noodles and fry until lightly brown, stirring constantly; place noodles on a paper towel to drain off excess oil.

In a medium bowl, combine noodles with the brown sugar and chocolate sprinkles, toss to mix. Roll each ice cream scoop in mixture and serve. Makes 4 servings.

CHOCO-BANANA CRUNCH CAKES

4	**individual-size sponge cakes**
1	**large banana,** sliced
¹/₃ cup	**maraschino cherries**
1 package	**any flavor ramen noodles,** crushed
1 cup	**hot fudge sauce,** warmed

Place sponge cakes on individual dessert dishes. Evenly distribute banana slices and cherries between cakes. Sprinkle noodles evenly over cakes and top with hot fudge. Makes 4 servings.

CHOCOLATE RAMEN

2 cups	**water**
I cup	**brown sugar**
I package	**any flavor ramen noodles**
I teaspoon	**vanilla**
I cup	**chocolate syrup**

In a medium saucepan, bring water and brown sugar to a boil. Add noodles and cook for 3 minutes. Reserve I tablespoon water and then drain noodles. Add remaining ingredients and reserved water. Toss and serve. Makes I serving.

STRAWBERRY
RAMEN ICE CREAM

4 scoops	**vanilla ice cream**
1 cup	**strawberry sauce**
1 package	**any flavor ramen noodles,** finely crushed

Place ice cream in individual dessert bowls. Top with strawberry sauce and sprinkle with noodles. Makes 4 servings.

CARAMEL RAMEN

¹/₂ cup	**butter or margarine**
¹/₂ cup	**brown sugar**
¹/₈ teaspoon	**vanilla**
1 tablespoon	**corn syrup**
1 package	**any flavor ramen noodles,** finely crushed

Preheat oven to 300 degrees. Liberally prepare a baking sheet with nonstick cooking spray.

In a small saucepan, mix the butter, brown sugar, vanilla, and corn syrup over medium heat until it starts to bubble and thicken, stirring often; remove from heat. Add noodles and toss to mix. Pour the mixture onto baking sheet and put in the oven for 4 minutes. Remove from the oven and cool in the fridge or freezer. Slice and serve. Makes 10–15 servings.

WHITE CHOCOLATE
RAMEN COOKIE

2 tablespoons	**butter or margarine**
3 packages	**any flavor ramen noodles,** crushed
1 package (12 ounces)	**white chocolate chips**
$1/4$ cup	**chopped macadamia nuts**

In a large frying pan, melt butter over medium heat. Add noodles and cook until lightly brown. Melt white chocolate chips in microwave or over a double broiler. Mix the browned noodles and nuts into the melted chocolate. Drop by tablespoonfuls onto wax paper and let set for 20 minutes. Makes 35–40 balls.

THIN MINT ON A STICK

1 bag (8 ounces)	**dark chocolate chips**
6 drops	**peppermint extract**
1 drop	**spearmint extract**
1 drop	**wintergreen extract**
2 packages	**any flavor ramen noodles,** crushed
12	**craft sticks**

In a medium saucepan or double boiler, melt the chocolate chips until they become smooth and creamy. Slowly add extracts to the chocolate. Stir for 1 minute. Add noodles and stir vigorously until completely covered. Using a tablespoon, immediately spoon mixture onto wax paper in round cookie shapes. Mixture will flatten and spread considerably, so leave lots of space in between. Place craft stick in each and chill in refrigerator until solid, about 1 hour. Makes 12.

NOTES

METRIC CONVERSION CHART

Volume Measurements		Weight Measurements		Temperature Conversion	
U.S.	Metric	U.S.	Metric	Fahrenheit	Celsius
1 teaspoon	5 ml	$1/2$ ounce	15 g	250	120
1 tablespoon	15 ml	1 ounce	30 g	300	150
$1/4$ cup	60 ml	3 ounces	90 g	325	160
$1/3$ cup	75 ml	4 ounces	115 g	350	180
$1/2$ cup	125 ml	8 ounces	225 g	375	190
$2/3$ cup	150 ml	12 ounces	350 g	400	200
$3/4$ cup	175 ml	1 pound	450 g	425	220
1 cup	250 ml	$2 1/4$ pounds	1 kg	450	230

 Check out these "101" favorites
for more tasty recipes:

Cake Mix	**Slow Cooker**
More Cake Mix	**More Slow Cooker**
Chocolate	**BBQ**
Gelatin	**Dutch Oven**
Yogurt	**Blender**
Pudding	**Toaster Oven**
Mac & Cheese	**Chicken**
Ramen Noodles	**Rotisserie Chicken**
Salad	**Ground Beef**
Zucchini	**Meatballs**
Tofu	**Grits**
Tortilla	**Potato**
Canned Biscuits	**Cheese**
Canned Soup	**Eggs**
Casserole	

Each 128 pages, $9.99

Available at bookstores or directly
from GIBBS SMITH
1.800.835.4993
www.gibbs-smith.com

ABOUT THE AUTHOR

Toni Patrick is the culinary creative behind *101 Things to Do with Ramen Noodles*, *101 Things to Do with Mac and Cheese*, *101 Things to Do with Canned Biscuits*, *101 Things to Do with a Blender*, and *101 Things to Do with Eggs*. She has been featured on the Food Network and lives in Walden, Colorado, with her daughter, Robbi.